20813

Contents

Introduction

Adapting and interpreting skills and effects from other crafts has long been the norm for enthusiastic cake decorators. The designs in this book make use of folding, frilling and pleating techniques associated with dressmaking and furnishing.

Intent on expanding the boundaries of sugarcraft, I, like many others, see all around me shapes, textures and effects that inspire me; my long-standing love of fashion has helped me create the cakes in this book. Step-by-step photographs and detailed instructions together show you how to achieve stunning new effects with folds and frills.

Equipment

Frilling and folding techniques can be carried out with quite basic equipment, but there are some items that will help you achieve better results: non-stick rolling pin and board; selection of paintbrushes; cranked palette knife; craft knife or scalpel; scriber; thin card for templates; thin bamboo skewers; soft sponge or foam; non-stick baking paper; thin-bladed scissors; piping bags; piping tubes; Garrett frill cutter; frilling tools; icing ruler; cellophane sheet or plastic food wrap; ball modelling tool.

Where specific cutters and tools are required, details are given with the relevant cake design.

Basic Recipes

Modelling Paste

The paste used throughout this book is modelling paste. It is made by kneading together a mixture of flower paste (gum paste) and sugarpaste. The type of flower paste you use will be a matter of personal preference; there are many good commercial varieties that are suitable, or you can make your own. The ratio of flower paste to sugarpaste can be varied considerably, though it is not recommended to use more than 50 per cent flower paste.

For firm modelling paste, use a half-and-half mixture of sugarpaste and flower paste. For a softer paste,

Sugar Inspirations

Folds & Frills

LINDA PAWSEY

Dedication

This book is dedicated with love to
my Mum, Nora, an enthusiastic
mentor and constant friend.

Published 1995 by Merehurst Limited
Ferry House, 51–57 Lacy Road, Putney,
London SW15 1PR

Editor: Helen Southall
Design: Rita Wüthrich
Photography by Alan Marsh
CEO & Publisher: Anne Wilson
International Sales Director: Kevin Lagden

Typeset by Servis Filmsetting Ltd, Manchester
Colour separation by P & W Graphics Pty Ltd, Singapore
Printed in Italy by Milanostampa SpA

make a mixture that is two-thirds sugarpaste and one-third flower paste. Firm modelling paste is best used for free-standing decorations and heavy swags, when a strong paste which will set quite hard is required. Soft modelling paste is most suitable for pleating and frilling as it does not dry out as quickly as the firm paste. It is especially good when pleating larger pieces of paste.

Glycerine added to both soft and firm paste immediately before rolling out maintains elasticity and prevents cracking. One or two drops per 30g (1oz) of paste should be sufficient.

Sugarpaste Glue

Sugarpaste glue is more suitable than water for attaching folds and frills because it does not dry out as quickly as water, so allowing longer to position finished pieces accurately.

Break 60g (2oz) sugarpaste into small pieces, and put it in a small heatproof bowl with 2½ tablespoons water. Heat in a microwave or over a saucepan of hot water, stirring occasionally, until the sugarpaste has completely dissolved. Store in a clean container. To use the 'glue', brush a little on to finished pieces with a fine paintbrush.

Tip

For dusting surfaces when rolling out paste, use a small sterilized muslin bag filled with a 50/50 mixture of icing sugar and cornflour.

Pleated Birthday Cake

This delicately coloured cake is completely covered in pleated modelling paste.

Try to keep your pleating as even as possible

for the most professional finish.

Materials
625g (1¼lb) soft lilac
modelling paste
(see page 4)
Dusting bag
(see page 5)
10x15cm (4x6 inch)
oval cake
Apricot glaze
500g (1lb)
almond paste
Glycerine
Sugarpaste glue
(see page 5)
Lilac and green ribbon
to trim board

Equipment
18x23cm (7x9 inch)
oval cake board
Thin card
Paintbrush

Sugar flowers
2 alstroemeria
4 sprays of ivy
2 scabious
8 small white filler
flowers
6 small white buds
4 green and 4 gold
1.5mm wired ribbon
loops

Preparing the cake
1 Cover the cake board with soft modelling paste and leave for 2 days. Brush the cake with apricot glaze. Cover with almond paste. Leave to dry for 24 hours. Secure the cake to the board with royal icing.

Side pleating
2 Make a thin card template 20cm (8 inches) long and as wide as the depth of the cake. Knead two drops of glycerine into 30g (1oz) modelling paste. Roll out to 1.75mm (¹⁄₁₆ inch) thick and cut to the size of the template.

3 Pleat the piece of paste following the instructions on pages 19–20. Attach to the side of the cake with glue. Repeat this procedure all around the cake.

Top pleating
4 Pleat another 20cm (8 inch) piece and cut it in half lengthways. With the cut edge on the inside, attach to the top outside edge of the cake. Repeat to complete the oval.

5 Roll out a further 20cm (8 inch) piece and cut it in half lengthways before pleating. Pleat each half, then cut again lengthways. Attach to the inside of the cake top, overlapping the cut edge of the outer sections.

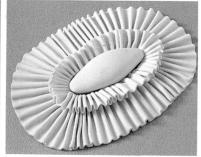

Finishing
6 Mould a ball of paste into a cigar shape to fit the centre of the cake top. Arrange the flowers in this and secure to the cake. Attach a smaller spray to the board.

Christening Cake

This pretty cake is coloured in pastel shades

of pink, but would be equally effective in blue, yellow or the palest green.

The bib can be decorated with any design you choose.

Materials
20cm (8 inch)
round cake
Apricot glaze
1kg (2lb) almond paste
Clear alcohol (gin or
vodka) for brushing
1.25kg (2½lb)
sugarpaste
Small quantity of
pale pink royal icing
125g (4oz) soft pink
modelling paste
(see page 4)
Dusting bag
(see page 5)
Sugarpaste glue
(see page 5)

1 **Preparing the cake**
Brush the cake with apricot glaze and cover with the almond paste. Leave to dry. Brush the almond paste with alcohol, and cover the cake and board with sugarpaste. Allow to dry for 3 days. Secure the cake to the board with royal icing.

2 **Side decoration**
Measure the depth and circumference of the cake and make a template from non-stick paper. Fold the paper into eight equal sections, and trace the design on page 11 on to each section. Make sure that all pencil lines are on the same side of the paper.

3 Attach the template to the cake using masking tape to join the ends, and scribe the design on to the cake. Remove the template.

4 With pale pink royal icing in a bag fitted with a no. 1 tube, pipe over the design on the cake sides.

5 Roll out a small quantity of pink modelling paste and cut out four small bows with a small bow cutter. With a three-petal broderie anglaise cutter, cut four sets of three petals. (These will form the tiny balloons.) Attach the bows and balloons around the cake as shown in the design on page 11.

6 **Base pleating**
Trace the oblong shape on page 47 on to greaseproof or non-stick paper and use to make a thin card template. Roll out a piece of pink modelling paste and cut three strips using the card template. Place the pieces under cellophane or plastic wrap to prevent drying out. Pleat each strip following the instructions on pages 19–20, then cut in half lengthways.

7 Using sugarpaste glue, secure each of these narrow pleated sections around the base of the cake, cutting and pleating further strips if they are required.

Bib

8 Cut a 7.5cm (3 inch) circle from rolled-out pink modelling paste. Use the same cutter to cut out a small section from the top of the bib.

9 Following the instructions in step 6, cut and pleat one strip of modelling paste, cut it in half lengthways, then slightly flatten the cut edges with the end of a paintbrush. Attach to the underside of the bib with glue. Emboss the top of the bib edge to neaten.

Equipment
28cm (11 inch)
round cake board
Masking tape
Scriber
Piping bags
Plain piping tube (no. 1)
Small bow cutter
Broderie anglaise cutter
Thin card
Icing ruler
Sheet of cellophane or
plastic food wrap
12x25cm (5x10 inch)
piece of soft sponge
or foam
Bamboo skewers
Paintbrush
7.5cm (3 inch)
ring cutter
Embossing tool
Petal cutter

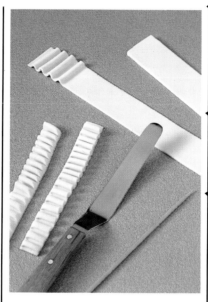

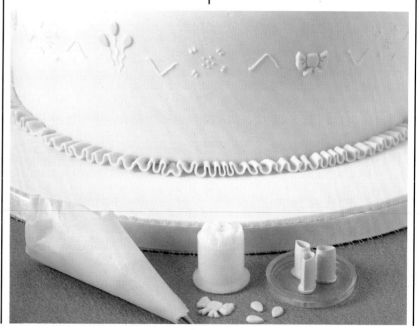

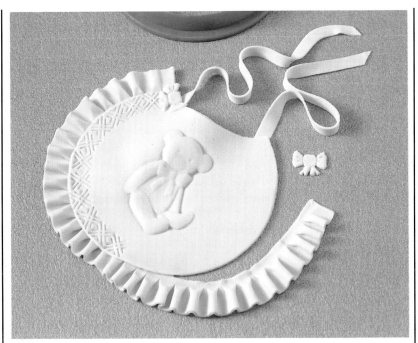

Finishing

10 Secure the bib to the cake top with glue, lifting the bib slightly in the centre. Attach thin strips of paste 10cm (4 inches) long for neck ribbons and a small bow on either side. The name is piped on to pink balloons cut from paste using a large petal or small round cutter.

11 The teddy bear on the bib was created using a mould taken from a child's brooch. Although moulds are available from cake-decorating shops, it is quite easy to make them yourself from brooches, fridge magnets, etc., avoiding items with eye holes or similar cut-out sections. Take an impression from the brooch by pressing it into a thick piece of neatly cut flower paste and allow this to harden thoroughly. To use, cut out the bib shape and press it gently on to the hardened mould which should first be dusted with a dusting bag (see page 5). A more permanent mould can be made from a non-toxic modelling material.

Autumn Splendour

This elegantly decorated cake is perfect for a fiftieth or sixtieth birthday celebration,

or for any birthday in the later months of the year.

If possible, use a real chinese lantern as a colour guide.

Materials

20x25cm (8x10 inch)
oval cake
Apricot glaze
1.5kg (3lb)
almond paste
Clear alcohol (gin or
vodka) for brushing
2kg (4lb) sugarpaste
Small quantity
of royal icing
Egg yellow and chestnut
brown food colourings
Piping gel
Nasturtium or
tangerine, brown and
white dusting powders
125g (4oz) firm
modelling paste
(see page 4)
Dusting bag
(see page 5)
Sugarpaste glue
(see page 5)
Cream-coloured ribbon
to trim board

Preparing the cake

1 Brush the cake with apricot glaze and cover with the almond paste. Leave to dry. Brush with alcohol, and cover the cake and board with sugarpaste. Leave to dry for 3 days. Secure the cake to the board with royal icing.

Side decoration

2 Measure the depth and circumference of the cake and make a template of non-stick paper. Fold into four quarters. In the centre of each section, trace the chinese lantern design on page 15, making sure that all pencil lines are on the same side of the template. Attach the template around the cake with masking tape.

3 Using the point of a scriber, mark the outlines of the design in four places on the sides of the cake, scratching the surface lightly. Remove the template.

4 Make another template of the top of the cake, fold into four equal sections and repeat the lantern design but only on to three of the four sections.

5 Colour a small quantity of royal icing with egg yellow and a touch of chestnut brown (use a real chinese lantern for reference). Add a little piping gel and use to fill a piping bag fitted with a no. 1 tube. Pipe round the outlines of the lanterns, then brush embroider them, using a damp paintbrush. Keep the colour as even as possible as you brush it across each flower.

6 Mix together some nasturtium or tangerine powder colour and a little chestnut or nut brown. Dilute this with either white powder colour or cornflour. (Try to mix to a similar colour to the royal icing used to brush embroider the lanterns.)

7 Roll out a small quantity of modelling paste and cut some lace pieces with a lace cutter. Frill with a silk effect modelling tool and brush lightly with the dusting powder. (Retain the rest of the colour for use later.) While still soft, attach to the base of the cake with glue.

8 Roll out and cut a 7.5cm (3 inch) square of modelling paste. Following the instructions on pages 19–20, pleat the square.

9 Trace the large fan shape on page 15 and use to make a template of thin card. Lay the template on the pleated square and cut out a fan of pleated modelling paste. Remove the template and pinch the pleated paste together at the base to join the pleats.

10 Repeat steps 8 and 9 until you have pleated and cut two large, two medium and two small fan shapes. Leave to dry for 24 hours. Dust with the remaining powder colour.

11 Stand one of each size of the fan shapes in a small ball of modelling paste with the largest at the back. Repeat with the remaining three.

Finishing
12 Arrange the leaves, lanterns and berries, etc., around the base of the fans, and then secure one arrangement to the cake board and one on the top of the cake in the quarter that does not have a lantern design. Trim the cake board with cream-coloured ribbon.

Equipment
28x33cm (11x13 inch)
oval cake board
Masking tape
Scriber
Piping bags
Plain piping tube (no. 1)
Paintbrushes
Lace cutter
Silk effect
modelling tool
Icing ruler
Thin card
Soft foam or sponge pad
Bamboo skewers

Sugar flowers
7 chinese lanterns
5 wheat heads
4 fungi
6 sprays
of green bud stamen
3 twigs
8 medium rose leaves
5 small rose leaves
5 rose hips
7 wired green
ribbon loops

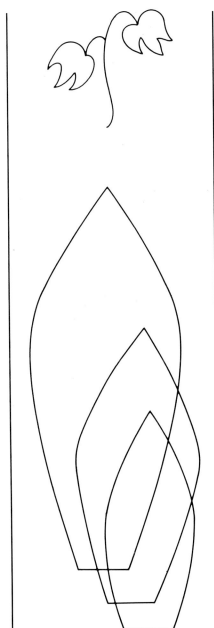

15

Valentine Cake

This beautiful heart-shaped cake could also be used for an engagement or wedding

The decorative pleating on the top and sides forms the perfect surround

for miniature red roses and rose buds.

Materials

2kg (4lb) cream
sugarpaste
25cm (10 inch)
heart-shaped cake
Apricot glaze
1.5kg (3lb)
almond paste
Clear alcohol (gin or
vodka) for brushing
Small quantity
of royal icing
Green ribbon
to trim cake
Sugarpaste glue
(see page 5)
125g (4oz) soft cream
modelling paste
(see page 4)
Dusting bag
(see page 5)
Pink food dusting
powder
Cream ribbon
to trim board

Sugar flowers

5 miniature red roses
4 miniature
red rose buds
16 tiny rose leaves

Preparing the cake

1 Cover the cake board with sugarpaste and allow to dry. Brush the cake with apricot glaze and cover with the almond paste. When dry, brush with alcohol and cover the cake with sugarpaste. Set aside to dry for 3 days. Secure the cake to the board with royal icing.

2 Cut a strip of non-stick paper that is as wide as the depth of the cake and long enough to wrap around the outer edge of the cake. Fold into four equal sections. Starting 5cm (2 inches) in from each fold and at a point halfway up the width of the template, trace the design shown on page 18 on to each quarter. (As the hearts are to be made of paste and fixed to the cake sides separately, mark their position with a dot only.) Ensure that all pencil lines are on one side of the template paper only so you can prevent them coming into contact with the cake.

3 Attach the template around the cake, securing with masking tape. Using the point of a scriber, mark the design on to the cake and remove the template.

Side piping

4 Using white royal icing in a piping bag fitted with a no. 1 tube, pipe the linework design on to the cake sides. Change to a no. 2 tube and pipe a snailstrail around the base of the cake. Attach the green ribbon about 1cm (½ inch) above the snailstrail with sugarpaste glue.

33cm (13 inch)
heart-shaped
cake board
Masking tape
Scriber
Piping bags
Plain piping tubes
(nos. 1 and 2)
Paintbrush
Thin card
12x25cm (5x10 inch)
piece of soft sponge
or foam
Bamboo skewers
Tiny heart cutter

Pleating

5 Roll out some modelling paste and cut out a square using the small template on page 47. Following the instructions on page 19, commence pleating, starting with the skewers across two of the corners in a diamond shape.

6 When complete, gently squeeze the pleats together in the centre. Make three more pieces using the same template. Attach a rose and two leaves to each and secure to the cake. Position one each side between the linework, one in the centre of the back, and one at the front.

Top decoration

7 For the top decoration, roll out some modelling paste and use the large template on page 47 to cut out a square. Halve the square diagonally, pleat each piece and gently squeeze together, coaxing one side into a slight curve.

8 Cut and pleat one more section using the small template and, while it is still soft, secure it to the top of the two larger pieces.

Finishing

9 Secure the remaining rose to the centre of the top piece of pleating with two buds either side. Arrange the rest of the leaves in a symmetrical design.

10 Tiny pink-dusted cut-out hearts positioned above and below the linework complete the cake. Brush the backs of the hearts with a little sugarpaste glue and press them gently on to the cake. Trim the board.

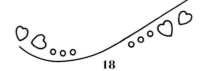

Pleating Techniques

Re-creating pleating on a cake adds a stunning new dimension to the decoration and a very effective background for sprays of flowers and foliage. It is valuable to practise the technique before attempting a cake, as pleating quickly is important to achieve good results. The elasticity of the modelling paste is vital and the addition of glycerine is useful as it delays the drying time long enough to prevent the pleats from cracking (see page 5).

Materials
Soft modelling paste
(see page 4)
Dusting bag
(see page 5)

Equipment
$13x20$cm ($5x8$ inch)
piece of soft sponge or
foam
Cake card
Thin card
Icing ruler
Craft knife or scalpel
2 bamboo skewers

1 Glue the piece of soft foam or sponge to a cake card. It is useful to work with the card on a non-slip surface as the pressure needed to pleat the paste sometimes causes the foam to move.

2 To achieve delicate pleats it is important to roll out the modelling paste quite thinly and to work as quickly as possible. Use a thin card template for specific shapes (see pages 46–47) or rectangles cut to the depth of the cake.

3 Roll out the paste on a lightly dusted board and lay your template on it. An icing ruler positioned along the edge of the template as a cutting guide will ensure the paste is cut cleanly. Do not cut a section longer than about 20cm (8 inches) as it will dry out too quickly. Transfer the piece of paste to the foam pad.

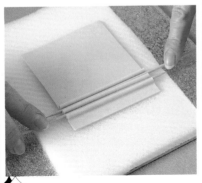

4 To begin pleating, hold a skewer in each hand, and commence at the top of the paste. Press both skewers down into the paste firmly. When the paste is forced in between, press them together to form a pleat.

Creative Pleating

Pleated sections and strips have a wide variety of uses both on and off cakes. If you use firm modelling paste (see page 4) for pleated strips on free-standing decorations, the decoration will hold its shape and dry to a hard finish.

With practice, you will soon be able to pleat quite long strips of rolled paste and attempt large decorations with fewer joins. When attaching one strip of pleated paste to another, brush on a little sugar-paste glue and overlap the ends slightly. Thin the overlapped pieces by rolling with the end of a paint-brush. This will neaten the join and, with care, make it inconspicuous.

5 Repeat the process along the length of the paste to complete the pleating.

Heart cake decoration
A thin pleated strip rolled flat on one side can be attached between two pastillage heart shapes (template opposite). Allow to dry flat for at least 3 days.

Secure the dried heart to a base using a ball of modelling paste. Arrange sugar flowers in the paste to make a beautiful decoration for the top of a wedding cake.

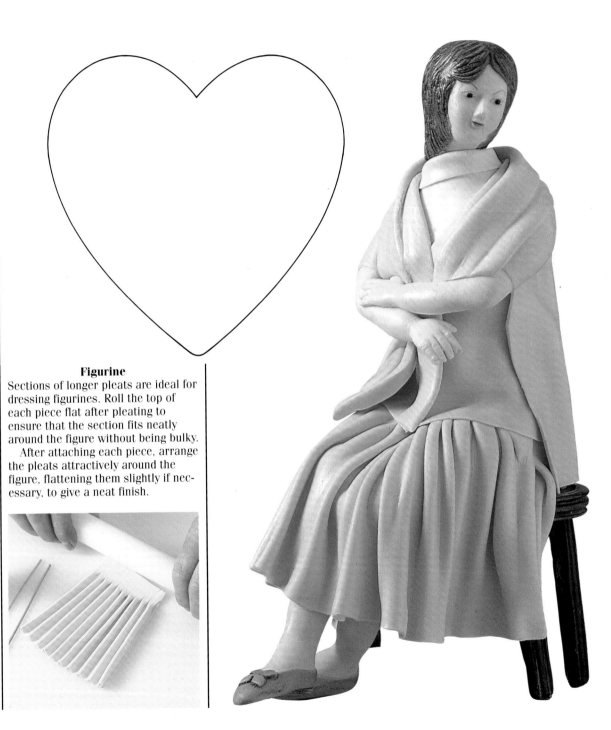

Figurine

Sections of longer pleats are ideal for dressing figurines. Roll the top of each piece flat after pleating to ensure that the section fits neatly around the figure without being bulky.

After attaching each piece, arrange the pleats attractively around the figure, flattening them slightly if necessary, to give a neat finish.

Strawberries and Cream

This delightful cake is suitable for a variety of summer celebrations.

Its folded trimmings give it a neat finish – and they couldn't be simpler to make.

Vary the colours and flowers you use to suit the occasion.

Materials

20cm (8 inch)
hexagonal cake
Apricot glaze
1kg (2lb) almond paste
Clear alcohol (gin or
vodka) for brushing
1.5kg (3lb) sugarpaste
royal icing
Green food colouring
125g (4oz)
soft modelling paste
(see page 4)
Dusting bag
(see page 5)
Sugarpaste glue
(see page 5)

Equipment

28cm (11 inch)
hexagonal cake board
Scriber
Piping bags
Plain piping tube (no. 1)
Paintbrush
7.5cm (3 inch)
ring cutter

Decorations

12 tiny strawberries
5 cream roses
6 moulded strawberries

1 **Preparing the cake**
Brush with apricot glaze and cover with almond paste. Leave to dry. Brush with alcohol, and cover cake and board with sugarpaste. Allow to dry for 3 days. Secure the cake to the board with royal icing.

2 **Side decoration**
Cut two pieces of non-stick paper the size of one side of the cake. Trace the design above on to one. Turn this tracing over and trace the design again on to the second template the opposite way round. Hold one template against one side of the cake, and scribe on the design, marking the position of the strawberries with a pin-prick only.

3 Change templates and mark the next side so the design flows up and down around the cake. With a no. 1 tube and green royal icing, pipe in the design. Attach strawberries.

4 **Folding**
Roll out some modelling paste and cut a strip 2.5cm (1 inch) wide. Fold the strip following the instructions on pages 24–25.

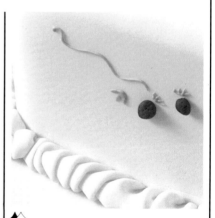

5 Turn the folded strip over and fold in half lengthways. Trim, and fix around the base of the cake with glue. Repeat around the cake.

6 Repeat steps 4–5 and attach two folded strips to the top of the cake in a circle. Use a 7.5cm (3 inch) ring cutter to hold until dry.

7 **Finishing**
Arrange flowers and strawberries in a ball of paste on top of the cake, adding leaves, filler flowers, gypsophila and wired ribbons as required.

Folding Techniques

Folding rather than pleating paste gives a much more random finish and has many applications. Use soft modelling paste (see page 4) for basic folded decorations.

An exciting variety of wedding-cake ornaments can be made by folding firm modelling paste (see page 4) in different ways. Trimmings for cakes and plaques can also be made easily. A narrow strip gives a very dainty finish, while wider pieces have a much more striking effect.

Materials
Soft modelling paste
(see page 4)
Dusting bag
(see page 5)
Sugarpaste glue
(see page 5)

Equipment
Icing ruler
Craft knife or scalpel
Bamboo skewer
Paintbrush

1 Roll out a piece of soft modelling paste on a lightly dusted board and cut a length using an icing ruler pressed gently on to the paste as a guide. The ruler will also prevent the paste dragging when it is cut.

2 Slide a bamboo skewer under the top part of the paste, and lift a section. Holding the paste, press the skewer into the top of the paste to form two folds. Repeat the procedure down the length of the paste, leaving small but uneven gaps between the folds.

3 Press the paste lightly with your fingertips to flatten it a little. Turn the ends of the strip under so that strips can be joined neatly.

4 Turn the strip over and brush sugarpaste glue on to one side. Working from top to bottom, fold the strip in half lengthways, pressing so that the edges stick together.

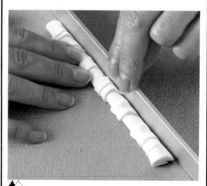

5 Press the cut edge of the folded section against the ruler to lift and roll the paste. Trim the cut edge with a sharp knife. Attach to cakes with sugarpaste glue while still soft.

Wedding-cake ornament

1 For the oval decoration shown below right, cut two ovals (one 10cm/4 inches long, the other 5cm/2 inches long) from firm modelling paste. Secure the smaller one on top of the larger and allow to dry.

2 Measure the distance around the edge of the base (about 25cm/11 inches) and cut a long strip of thin paste 1cm (½ inch) wide. Brush the strip with sugarpaste glue and fold the long edges into the middle. Press to seal. Brush one side with glue and fold the whole piece in half lengthways. Working as quickly as possible, twist the folded paste around and around until a 'rope' effect is achieved.

3 While still soft, attach the 'rope' to the edge of the base with glue, pressing gently to make sure that it binds.

4 For the upright oval shape, repeat the procedure, this time cutting a strip 5cm (2 inches) wide. Once twisted, brush the ends with glue and pinch together.

5 Lay the piece on a pad of soft sponge around the oval cutter to maintain the shape whilst drying. Allow to dry and harden for at least 48 hours.

6 When dry, attach the oval shape to the base using a ball of soft paste to hold it in position. This soft paste will also hold the flowers. A paste bow adds a delicate finish.

Plaques

The folded rope twist is very effective when used to edge plaques, especially if a coloured rope border is attached to a white plaque.

Follow the instructions for making a wide rope twist, as given in steps 2 and 4, left. Just before twisting the paste, colour the edges quickly. Twist the paste and attach to the edge of the plaque with sugarpaste glue while soft. Decorate with flowers pushed into a ball of soft modelling paste.

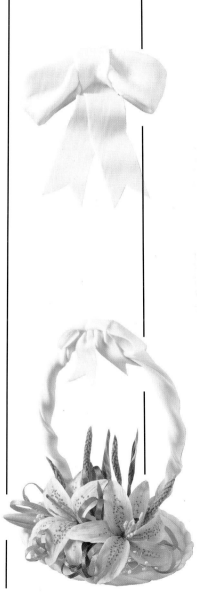

Oriental Theme

This unusual design for a celebration cake is inspired by Chinese brush painting techniques.

The brush embroidery work is easy to carry out, while the chrysanthemums

give depth to the finished design.

Materials

20x25cm (8x10 inch) oval cake
Apricot glaze
1.5kg (3lb) almond paste
Clear alcohol (gin or vodka) for brushing
2kg (4lb) sugarpaste
Royal icing
Claret, green and ivory food colourings
Piping gel
Ivory modelling paste for bamboo
Sugarpaste glue (see page 5)
125g (4oz) firm modelling paste (see page 4)
Dusting bag (see page 5)
3 claret chrysanthemums (see page 37)

Equipment

28x33cm (11x13 inch) oval cake board
Scriber
Piping bags
Plain piping tube (no. 1)
Paintbrushes
Frilling tool

Preparing the cake

1 Brush with apricot glaze and cover with almond paste. Leave to dry. Brush the cake with alcohol, and cover cake and board with sugarpaste. Dry for 3 days. Secure the cake to the board with royal icing.

Top decoration

2 Cut a piece of non-stick paper the size of the top of the cake, and trace on to it the leaves only from the design on page 46. Scribe the leaves on to the cake top. Colour a little royal icing green and add some piping gel. Using a no. 1 tube, pipe round the outlines, then brush embroider them. When dry, paint in veins. Attach the bamboo and chrysanthemums.

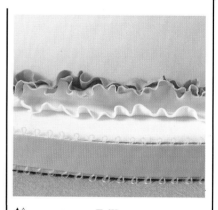

Frills

3 Roll a strip of firm modelling paste 1cm (½ inch) wide. Frill both long edges, then fold in half lengthways and attach to the cake board with glue. Ensure that the top half of the frill does not touch the cake. Repeat all around the cake.

4 Colour half the remaining modelling paste green. Roll out and cut a strip 5mm (¼ inch) wide. Frill on one side only. Brush the first frill with glue and attach the green one. Brush the frill down so that it follows the shape of the first frill. Attach green frills around the cake. Repeat, making a claret frill.

Lilac=time Wedding Cake

Lilac is the most appropriate colour scheme for a May wedding,

when lilac trees are blooming, but you can vary the colours used on this cake

to suit any time of year.

Materials

2.5kg (5lb) lilac
sugarpaste
18x28cm (7x11 inch)
and 15x23cm (6x9
inch) teardrop cakes
Apricot glaze
2kg (4lb) almond paste
Clear alcohol (gin or
vodka) for brushing
Sugarpaste glue
(see page 5)
Green and beige ribbon
Royal icing
Green food colouring
125g (4oz) soft lilac
modelling paste (see
page 4)

Equipment

23x33cm (9x13 inch)
and 20x28cm (8x11
inch) teardrop cake
boards
Texture tool
Scriber
Piping bag
Plain piping tube (no. 0)
Garrett frill cutter

Sugar flowers

10 lilac roses
7 sprays of lilac freesia

Preparing boards and cakes

1 Cover the cake boards with sugarpaste and mark the paste around the edges with a texture tool.

2 Brush the cakes with apricot glaze and cover with almond paste. Dry. Brush with alcohol and cover with sugarpaste. Dry for 3 days. Secure cakes to boards.

Side decoration

3 Scribe a line around the sides of the cakes 4cm (1½ inches) up from the base. Attach green ribbon around each cake, following the lines. Secure beige ribbon above the green.

4 Colour some royal icing green and fill a piping bag fitted with a no. 0 tube. Piping freehand, copy the design above on to the cake sides.

Base frills

5 Roll out some lilac modelling paste and cut out a circle with a Garrett frill cutter (with centre removed). Frill with a texture tool (see pages 32–33).

6 Brush around a section of the base of each cake with sugarpaste glue and attach the frill with the textured side uppermost. Gently curve the frill towards the board. Continue to roll, cut and frill further pieces until a first layer is completed around each cake.

7 Repeat steps 5–6 and attach a second layer of frills above the first around each of the two cakes.

8 Arrange the roses and freesia in two teardrop sprays, adding ivy, rose and fern leaves, dried gypsophila, wired ribbons and tulle (see page 44), as required.

28

Christmas Cake

This unusual Christmas cake uses simple jabot=style folded frills

to decorate the top of the cake. Shaped like Christmas trees, they are edged

with delicate piping.

Materials
20x25cm (8x10 inch)
scalloped oval cake
Apricot glaze
1.5kg (3lb)
almond paste
Clear alcohol (gin or
vodka) for brushing
2kg (4lb)
cream sugarpaste
Sugarpaste glue
(see page 5)
Green and gold ribbon
to trim cake
Red and green ribbon
to trim board
Small quantity
of royal icing
60g (2oz)
firm modelling paste
(see page 4)
Dusting bag
(see page 5)
Red, green and gold
food colourings

Preparing the cake
1 Brush the cake with apricot glaze and cover with the almond paste. Leave to dry. Brush the almond paste with alcohol, and cover the cake and board with sugarpaste. Allow to dry for 3 days. Secure the cake to the board with royal icing.

Side decoration
2 Scribe a line around the sides of the cake 2.5cm (1 inch) up from the base. Using sugarpaste glue, attach a length of green ribbon around the cake on the marked line. Attach another length 1cm (½ inch) above the first. Secure gold ribbon around the base of the cake. Trim the board with red and green ribbon.

3 At intervals of about 7.5cm (3 inches) around the cake, slightly above the green ribbons, attach a large holly leaf with royal icing. In between these leaves and this time below the ribbons, attach further large leaves.

4 Attach small leaves, berries and cones to complete the design. (Reserve 6 small leaves and berries.)

Stars
5 Roll out some modelling paste and cut out 30 small stars. Leave eight to dry. Attach the remainder with sugarpaste glue to the cake board. Paint the dried stars with gold food colouring and set aside to dry thoroughly.

Christmas trees
6 Roll out some more modelling paste and cut two 10cm (4 inch) circles and one 7.5cm (3 inch) circle. From each of the circles, cut out a 4cm (1½ inch) middle. Following the instructions on pages 32–33, form a jabot frill from each of the circles. Allow to dry.

Equipment
28x33cm (11x13 inch)
scalloped oval
cake board
Scriber
Icing ruler
Paintbrushes
Small star cutter
Set of ring cutters
Piping bags
2 plain piping tubes
(no. 0)

Decorations
18 large holly leaves
18 small holly leaves
24 holly berries
6 fir cones

7 Attach the 'trees' to the top of the cake with royal icing, positioning the small tree in the centre and the larger ones on either side.

8 Colour some royal icing red and green and fill two bags fitted with no. 0 tubes. Pipe green dots around the edges of the frills, and then in between fill in with red dots to form a continuous border.

Finishing
9 Attach three small holly leaves and three berries to either side of the top of the cake, and the gold stars above the Christmas trees, positioning one at the top of each.

10 Make small rectangles from modelling paste and use to form the tree trunks.

Note: Ensure that the gold stars are removed from the cake before serving as the colouring is inedible.

Frilling Techniques

Frills are a popular cake decoration. They can be used to make simple eye-catching finishes in a variety of textures and shapes. Soft or firm modelling paste (see page 4) can be used depending on the effect desired. With a variety of texture tools now available, it is possible to create a new look for the Garrett frill. The two-tier lilac wedding cake on page 29 shows what can be achieved.

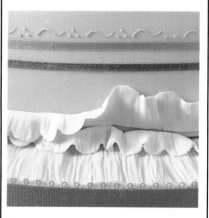

Garrett frill
1 On a lightly dusted board, roll out some *soft* modelling paste and cut a Garrett frill. With the tip of a texture tool, roll backwards and forwards around the outer edge of the circle of paste until it is completely frilled.

Jabot-style frill
2 A very elegant jabot-style frill can be achieved by cutting plain circles and folding the whole piece back and forth on itself. This effect can be used on the top or sides of a cake (see the cake on page 31).

3 Roll out a piece of *firm* modelling paste and cut a circle using a plain-edged ring cutter. (The size of the outer and inner circles depends on what effect is required.)

Materials
Dusting bag
(see page 5)
Soft modelling paste
(see page 4)
Firm modelling paste
(see page 4)

Equipment
Garrett frill cutter
Texture tools
Ring cutters
in various sizes
Frilling tools

4 Cut out a centre and, with a frilling tool, lightly soften around the outer edge.

Double-edged frill

6 Frilling both sides of a straight length of paste forms a delicate edging that can be used either around the sides of a cake or on a plaque.

7 Roll out some *soft* modelling paste and cut a strip of thin paste about 1cm (½ inch) wide. Dust the board lightly and frill along both sides of the piece. The frill is now ready to be applied.

Figurine

8 Frilled paste can be used to great advantage when dressing figures. The little doll in the picture has a dress, petticoat, apron and bonnet all made from frills.

5 Cut through the frill to form a strip. Fold one end under and repeat, working from side to side until a fluted cone shape is formed.

Peach Delight Wedding Cake

The flowers on this beautiful two-tier cake

are easily made from folded circles of modelling paste.

The leaves and beads are arranged in a 'cascade' over each cake to great effect.

Materials
20cm (8 inch)
round cake
15cm (6 inch)
round cake
Apricot glaze
1.5kg (3lb)
almond paste
Clear alcohol (gin or
vodka) for brushing
2kg (4lb)
peach sugarpaste
Wired strips of
small pearl beads
(see page 37)
Small quantity
of royal icing
185g (6oz) soft
peach modelling paste
(see page 4)
Dusting bag
(see page 5)
Sugarpaste glue
(see page 5)
Pale peach ribbon
to trim boards

Preparing the cakes
1 Brush the cakes with apricot glaze and cover with the almond paste. Leave to dry. Brush the almond paste with alcohol, and cover the cakes and boards with peach sugarpaste. Allow to dry for 3 days. Secure the cakes to the boards. Attach tiny strips of beads with royal icing to the base of each cake.

Roses
2 Roll out some peach modelling paste and cut out five 6cm (2½ inch) circles.

3 Place all the circles under cellophane or plastic wrap, removing them one at a time to form into petals as shown on page 37. Arrange the petals in a circle, overlapping the centres slightly, and glue together with sugarpaste glue.

4 Repeat steps 2 and 3, this time using a smaller 5cm (2 inch) ring cutter. Place these completed petals inside the larger five and secure with glue. Roll out and form a further three 5cm (2 inch) petals and place inside the inner group.

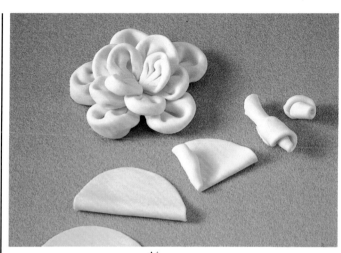

6 Repeat steps 2–5 to make two further roses.

Leaves and beads

7 Cut a variety of leaf sizes, also out of peach modelling paste. You will need about 24 large, 24 medium and 8 small leaves. Place the leaves on a pad of soft sponge or foam and use a ball tool to soften each leaf around the edges, with the tool completely on the leaf. Mark centre veins with a dresden tool.

8 For the beads, roll small balls of peach modelling paste.

Equipment
28cm (11 inch)
round cake board
20cm (8 inch)
round cake board
Set of ring cutters
Sheet of cellophane or
plastic food wrap
Paintbrush
Leaf cutters
Pad of soft sponge
or foam
Ball modelling tool
Dresden tool

5 For the centre cone, cut a 6cm (2½ inch) circle and roll (rather than gather) into a tight bud shape. Pinch off surplus paste. Make a slight indent in the middle of the flower and glue the centre in position.

Finishing

9 Attach the roses, leaves and beads in a cascading arrangement around the sides of the cakes. Trim the boards with peach ribbon.

Flowers, Leaves and Beads

A completely new look can be achieved for flowers and leaves by simply folding and pleating the paste. Soft modelling paste is used for flowers and firm modelling paste for leaves and beads. The size of flower is determined by the size of ring cutter used and the number of petals. The shape of the centre can also be changed to give variety, e.g. small pieces of paste pressed on to tulle or lace give an effective finish.

Beads

3 A variety of beads can be made from small balls of paste. After shaping and drying, these can be dusted with lustre powder or glazed. They can also be threaded on to 28 gauge wires and used in sprays just like real beads.

Flowers and leaves

1 On a lightly dusted board, roll out some soft modelling paste until quite thin. Cut different-sized circles. Fold each circle in half and bring both corners down and in to the centre to form petal shapes.

2 Flowers with thin petals, such as daisies and chrysanthemums, can be made by rolling some thin firm paste around a drinking straw or skewer. Slide the straw out and cut small sections of paste, holding the scissors at an angle of 45°. Individual leaves can also be made this way.

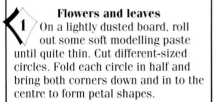

Materials
Dusting bag
(see page 5)
Soft modelling paste
(see page 4)
Firm modelling paste
(see page 4)
Sugarpaste glue
(see page 5)

Equipment
Set of ring cutters
Plastic drinking straw or
bamboo skewer
Scissors
28 gauge white wires

Celebration Cake

This elegant twenties-style cake is suitable for any occasion
that calls for something a little unusual. The swags and tails used to decorate it add
a touch of sophistication, making the cake appropriate for a small wedding.

Materials

20x25cm (8x10 inch)
oval cake
Apricot glaze
1.5kg (3lb)
almond paste
Clear alcohol (gin or
vodka) for brushing
2kg (4lb)
peach sugarpaste
Lace ribbon to trim cake
Sugarpaste glue
(see page 5)
250g (8oz) firm peach
modelling paste
(see page 4)
Green lustre food
dusting powder
Ribbon to trim board

Equipment

28x33cm (11x13 inch)
oval cake board
Masking tape
Scriber
Paintbrush
Thin card
Bamboo skewer
Scissors

Preparing the cake

1 Brush with apricot glaze and
cover with almond paste. Leave
to dry. Brush with alcohol, and cover
the cake and board with sugarpaste.
Leave to dry for 3 days. Secure the
cake to the board with royal icing.

2 Using non-stick paper, make a
template the depth and circumference of the cake and fold into six
equal sections. Mark a curve in the
top half of one of the sections and,
with the paper still folded, cut this
piece out. Attach the template around
the cake with masking tape. Scribe
the curves on to the cake sides.
Attach lace ribbon around the base.

Making the swags

3 Trace the larger template on
page 47 on to greaseproof or
non-stick paper and use to make a
thin card template. Roll out a piece of
modelling paste and use the template
to cut a swag. Following the instructions on page 41, fold and frill the
swag. Brush the back with sugarpaste glue and attach to the cake
side with the top fold along the
scribed curve. Make five more swags
and attach to the cake sides.

Making the tails

4 Use the small rectangle on page
47 to make a template. Roll out
a small piece of modelling paste and
cut around the template.

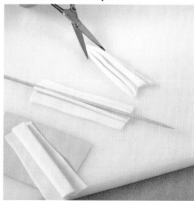

5 Place a skewer under the piece
lengthways and raise the centre.
Press the paste together under the
skewer. Remove the skewer and
press it on top of the fold to form two
pleats. Cut a 'V' shape out of one end
and cut the other end at an angle
with scissors. Make five further tails.
Attach one to where the swags join.

6 For the beads, roll balls of modelling paste.

8 Fold over both ends so they meet in the middle. Glue and pinch together. Cut a strip of paste about 10cm (4 inches) long and wrap it around the bow. Repeat to make two bows.

Finishing
9 The flowers are arranged in a ball of paste in the centre of the top of the cake with a bow attached on either side.

10 Dust the round beads with green lustre powder and attach to the sides of the cake, above each tail, with sugarpaste glue.

Making the bows
7 Roll out and cut a rectangle of modelling paste using the large template made for the swags. Fold over both long sides and make a tuck lengthways down the centre.

11 Trim the board with ribbon.

Sugar flowers
2 green
cymbidium orchids
8 ribes
6 fern leaves
3 sprays of green
dried gypsophila
3 wired
peach ribbon loops
4 medium and 4 small
ribes leaves

Swags

Gently draped around the sides of a cake, swags add a wonderful dimension to cake decorating with endless possibilities. Several different styles of swags can be made by folding and frilling the paste in different ways. Fashion, curtains, hats and furnishings are an endless source of inspiration for new designs that can be adapted to sugarcraft.

Using firm modelling paste helps to maintain the shape of the swags, and to prevent sagging once they are attached to the cake. The addition of glycerine to the paste immediately before rolling out helps to stop the folded paste cracking.

To achieve a neat finish, it is important to use a template and to scribe the design on to the cake. This will ensure accurate positioning of the swags which is particularly important when there is more than one tier.

As with pleating, the quicker the paste is folded the less chance there is of the surface of the paste cracking, so practise several times before attempting the swags on a cake.

1 Using non-stick paper, make a template the depth and circumference of the cake, and fold it into equal sections. This may be four, six or eight, depending on how many swags you wish to have on the cake.

2 Mark a curve on the top section of the template, then cut away the top part through all sections. Attach the template around the cake with masking tape and transfer the curved outline on to the sides with

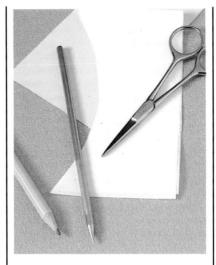

the point of a scriber. (The swags do not all need to be the same size, and the positioning on the cake side may vary, but the cake must look balanced and neat.)

3 Using the first template as a guide, cut a rectangle of thin card that is about the length of one of the curves and at least twice the depth required for the finished swag.

4 On a lightly dusted board, roll out a piece of firm modelling paste (the size of the piece will vary in accordance with the size of swag required). Cut a rectangle of paste using the card template.

5 Fold one long side of the rectangle over 1cm (½ inch). Slide a skewer under the centre and lift. With finger and thumb, press the paste together, then remove the skewer.

Materials
Dusting bag
(see page 5)
Firm modelling paste
(see page 4)
Sugarpaste glue
(see page 5)

Equipment
Scissors
Masking tape
Scriber
Thin card
Craft knife or scalpel
Icing ruler
Bamboo skewers
Paintbrush

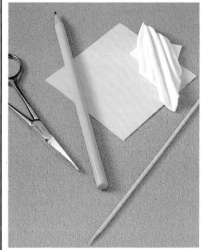

Tails

When using swags on cakes, a tail or similar decoration is often used to cover the point where two swags are joined.

Using the pleating and folding techniques described earlier in this book, a wide variety of tails can be made. Firm or soft modelling paste can be used, depending on the intricacy of the design.

Pleated tails

1 Cut a thin card template 7.5cm (3 inches) square. Roll out a small piece of paste on a lightly dusted board and use the template to cut a square.

6 Gently flatten the fold a little with your fingers, then with the skewer to form two pleats. The bottom edge may be either folded under or frilled (see page 32).

7 Pinch the swag at either end to gather up the folds and curve slightly ready to go on the cake.

8 Brush the back of the swag with sugarpaste glue and attach to the cake side, following the curve marked on the cake with the scriber.

2 Following the instructions on pages 19–20, pleat the paste, working from corner to corner. Squeeze the pleats together at the top. With scissors held at an angle of 45°, cut the paste to neaten.

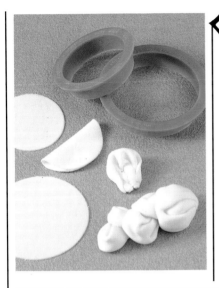

Folded tails

3 Using folded circles of varying sizes, make petal shapes similar to those shown on page 37. Press each slightly so that they can be attached to one another.

Shown below is a selection of the types of decorations that can be used as tails. For instructions for making the bow and simple folded tail, see pages 38 and 40. It is advisable to attach the tails with sugarpaste glue while they are still soft so that they can be moulded over the swags.

For brightly coloured tails, two colours of paste can be rolled together before pleating. Paste can also be textured or frilled to vary the finish.

Materials
Modelling paste
(see page 4)
Dusting bag
(see page 5)
Sugarpaste glue
(see page 5)

Equipment
Thin card
Scissors
Craft knife or scalpel
Bamboo skewers
Ring cutters

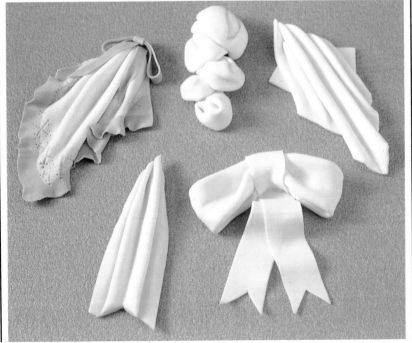

Tulle and Ribbon Techniques

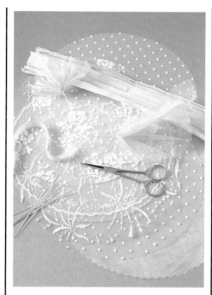

Decorative frills and folds can also be made from tulle, lace and the stiff paper ribbons that are used in floristry.

A vast array of designs and colours is available in the tulle and lace circles which are used for the almond favours so popular at weddings nowadays.

The tulle and lace circles can be wired and trimmed into small frills and incorporated into sprays of sugar or silk flowers to give a light and airy touch.

Tulle is also a subtle way of covering up the paste that holds the flowers in position.

The tulle circles normally available are about 23cm (9 inches) in diameter. To form frills, cut a circle in half. Bring together the middle and hook a wire round, twisting until the tulle is firmly gathered. Trim the edges in a semi-circle so that they follow the contours of the spray. It is also quite easy to trim the tulle further once it is actually incorporated into the spray.

When using tulle, lace or ribbon in flower sprays, it is advisable to use them sparingly – two or three pieces of wired tulle in even a large spray will enhance the flowers and foliage, while more could detract from the focal point, the flowers. In a floral arrangement for a wedding cake, lace pieces the same as the lace used for the bride's dress or veil could be used to great effect.

As the selection of ribbons available increases, so the choice may be more difficult. The colour chosen should complement or match the flowers on the cake without overwhelming the finished arrangement.

Equipment
Stiff paper ribbon
Tulle and lace circles
White 28 gauge wires
White floral tape
Fine scissors

Stiff crinkled paper ribbon is very good for cutting into different shapes and giving height and depth to arrangements. Many garden centres stock a selection of colours and widths. To make fans and bows, first unfold the paper ribbon carefully (if necessary). To wire the ribbon, cut a piece of paper ribbon twice the finished length required. Fold in half and twist a piece of wire around the middle. Cut to the shape required.

Christening Cake
(page 8)

Pleating (page 19)
large template

Oriental Theme
(page 26)

Pleating (page 19)
small template

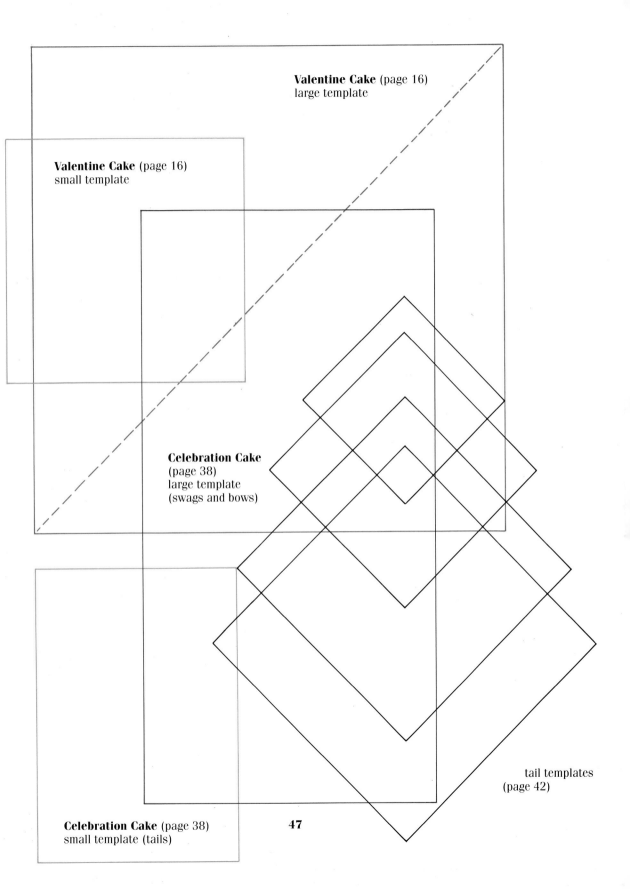

Valentine Cake (page 16)
large template

Valentine Cake (page 16)
small template

Celebration Cake
(page 38)
large template
(swags and bows)

47

tail templates
(page 42)

Celebration Cake (page 38)
small template (tails)

Acknowledgements

The author would like to thank the following for their help in the production of this book: George Hosgood and Terry Wood for their support and friendship; Debbie Welsh for her help.

The author would also like to thank the following for supplying equipment for photography:

D. I. Y. Icing Centre
(boards, dummies, boxes, stands, etc.),
8 Edwards Road, Erdington,
Birmingham B24 9EP
Tel & Fax: 0121-384 8236

J. F. Renshaw Ltd.
(Regalice),
Crown Street,
Liverpool L8 7RF
Tel: 0151-706 8200

Celcakes
(Celpads, etc.),
Springfield House,
Gate Helmsley,
York,
North Yorkshire YO4 1NF
Tel: 01759-371447

Holly Products
(texture tools),
Holly Cottage,
Hassall Green,
Sandbach,
Cheshire CW11 0YA
Tel: 01270-761403;
Fax: 01270-760068

The publishers would like to thank the following suppliers:

Cake Art Ltd.
Venture Way,
Crown Estate,
Priorswood,
Taunton, TA2 8DE
Tel: 01823 321532

Guy, Paul & Co. Ltd.
Unit B4,
Foundry Way,
Little End Road,
Eaton Socon,
Cambs. PE19 3JH
Tel: 01480 472545

Squires Kitchen
Squires House,
3 Waverley Lane,
Farnham,
Surrey GU9 8BB
Tel: 01252 711749

**Anniversary House
(Cake Decorations) Ltd.**
Unit 16,
Elliott Road,
West Howe Industrial Estate,
Bournemouth BH11 8LZ
Tel: 01202 590222